KEN GRIFFEY, JR.

THE KID

By Howard Reiser

CHILDRENS PRESS ®
CHICAGO

Photo Credits

Cover, ©Michael Ponzini/Focus On Sports; 6, AP/Wide World; 9, ©Otto Greule, Allsport USA; 10, Allsport USA; 11, AP/Wide World; 12, Allsport USA; 14, AP/Wide World; 17, UPI/Bettmann; 19, Focus On Sports; 20, Sportschrome East/West; 23, ©Ken Levine/Allsport USA; 25, ©Jonathan Daniel/Allsport USA: 27, ©Michael Ponzini/Focus On Sports; 28, Focus On Sports; 31, 32, AP/Wide World; 33, ©Jerry Wachter/Focus On Sports; 34, 37, 38, 39, AP/Wide World; 41, ©Otto Greule, Jr./Allsport USA; 42, ©Tom DiPace/Focus on Sports; 44, ©Rob Tringali, Jr./Sportschrome East/West

Project Editor: Shari Joffe
Design: Beth Herman Design Associates
Photo Research: Jan Izzo

Acknowledgments

The author would like to thank Ken Griffey, Jr., and Ken Griffey, Sr.; the public relations departments of the Seattle Mariners and the New York Yankees; Mariners pitching coach Sammy Ellis; Yankees hitting coach Frank Howard; Nylah Schneider of the New Hyde Park Public Library; and great baseball fan Derek Stark for their kind assistance in the development of this biography.

Library of Congress Cataloging-in-Publication Data

Reiser, Howard.
    Ken Griffey, Jr. (the kid) / by Howard Reiser.
      p. cm. – (Sports stars)
    ISBN 0-516-04384-6
    1. Griffey, Ken–Juvenile literature. 2. Baseball players–United States–Biography–Juvenile literature. [1. Griffey, Ken. 2. Baseball players. 3. Afro-Americans–Biography.] I. Title. II. Series.
GV865.G697R45   1994
796.357'092–dc20
   [B]   93-41054
                                                  CIP
                                                  AC

KEN GRIFFEY, JR.

THE KID

★ ★ ★

He wore a wide smile. He joked with his teammates and visitors. He was having a wonderful time.

His name is Ken Griffey, Jr. He is a great baseball player. That, alone, makes him special. But he is special also because of the immense joy he feels when playing baseball.

"I have always loved baseball," said Ken, chatting in the visitors' clubhouse at Yankee Stadium in New York City. "I am living out a beautiful dream. I always wanted to play in the major leagues. I am very happy with what I do, and with my accomplishments."

The Seattle Mariners have been equally happy with Ken, ever since he joined them as a nineteen-year-old rookie center fielder in 1989. At the time, he was the youngest player in the majors.

"He can run, throw, hit, and field," marveled Mariners pitching coach Sammy Ellis as he glanced at Ken in the clubhouse. "He can do everything. And he has wonderful enthusiasm. He could become one of the greatest players ever."

Ken, whose nickname is Junior, is proud of his talent. But he prefers not to call attention to himself, or discuss personal goals. "If a player talks a lot about himself, or about what he hopes to achieve, he could easily disappoint himself, and his team," Junior says. "Instead of playing relaxed, he might become tense trying to live up to his statements. This could prevent him from doing well. I just do my very best, have a lot of fun, and let things happen naturally."

Junior and his dad, Ken Griffey, Sr., in the dugout

While Junior spoke, his father sat at a nearby locker. Now the batting coach of the Mariners, Ken Griffey, Sr., had enjoyed his own successful major-league career. Toward the end of his career, he and Junior became the first father and son to play in the big leagues at the same time. Later, they became the first father and son to play together on the same team.

As the Mariners prepared for the opening of a three-game series against the Yankees, Ken Griffey, Sr., acknowledged his son's vast talent. But he added, "I don't want him to be concerned about impressing me, or anyone else. As long as he does the best he can, and continues to have fun, he will be just fine."

In the Yankees' locker room, Yankees coach Frank Howard spoke glowingly of the six-foot, three-inch Junior, who bats and throws left-handed. "Few players have had his all-around ability," said Howard. "A player like Ken comes along once in a million."

Junior was born on November 21, 1969, in Donora, Pennsylvania. His father, after playing nearly five years in the minor leagues, had just been drafted by the Cincinnati Reds. So Ken, Sr., and his wife, Alberta–known as Bertie–moved their family to Cincinnati.

Because of their father's career, Junior (left) and his brother Craig (right) have always been part of the world of major-league baseball.

Junior grew up around major-league baseball. He and his younger brother, Craig, would play with the children of Pete Rose and other players on the Reds. When visiting the Reds' clubhouse, Junior felt comfortable enough to grab cans of soda from manager Sparky Anderson's refrigerator.

Junior began playing baseball when he was seven years old. Two years later, he joined a Little League team. "My father always told me that no one was better than I was," Junior recalls.

Junior excelled in his very first year in Little League. He got a base hit every time up. He also had a pitching record of 12 wins and no losses.

The next season, Junior struck out for the first time. He stomped away angrily, behaving like a spoiled boy. "I calmed him down," recalls Junior's mother. "I reminded him that even his dad strikes out."

★ ★ ★

In 1981, when Junior was twelve years old, his father was traded by the Reds to the New York Yankees. Though the family continued to live in Cincinnati, Junior regularly visited New York during the baseball season. During Senior's five years with the Yankees, Junior often batted against his father in batting practice. "Once Junior reached the age of twelve, I could no longer strike him out," recalls his dad.

By the time Junior was fourteen, he had already begun to attract wide attention. Junior could hit the ball 400 feet, was a fast runner, and was an excellent outfielder.

Although Junior played a shallow center field, few balls were hit over his head. "I always felt I was better at going back on balls than at coming in," Junior explains.

Ken Griffey, Sr., as a New York Yankee in the early 1980s

★ ★ ★

Junior attended Moeller High School in Cincinnati. Because his grades were poor during his first two years, he was not allowed to participate in school sports. Junior understood that he would have to improve his marks if he wanted to play.

He began to play closer attention in class. He studied harder after school. Soon, his grades improved. In his junior year, he was finally allowed to participate in school sports. First he joined the football team, then the baseball team.

In football, he showed talent as a wide receiver, punter, and kicker. But he quit football after his junior season so he could concentrate on baseball. "All he talked about was baseball," says Griffey, Sr.

Junior playing baseball in high school

Junior did more than talk about baseball. On the field, there was no one better. Batting third and playing center field, he batted .478 in 28 games in his junior season. He also hit 10 home runs, drove in 33 runs, and made only 2 errors. He was voted Player of the Year.

The following season, he again batted .478. He hit 7 homers, drove in 23 runs, and was voted Player of the Year for the second straight season.

Unfortunately, Junior played poorly whenever his father attended his games. "He put too much pressure upon himself when I watched him," recalls Griffey, Sr. "I never saw him do much."

The Seattle Mariners, however, had seen Junior do enough to make him the first selection in the June 1987 amateur draft.

Junior was assigned to the Mariners' Rookie League team in Bellingham, Washington. Although he was only seventeen years old, Junior was immediately expected to play like a star. The fans buzzed excitedly every time Junior came up to bat. Even the park announcer added to the fun. "What time is it?" the announcer would bellow. "Griffey time," the crowd would answer.

Junior struggled early in the season. His poor start made him sad. "I told him to concentrate harder," recalled Junior's mom.

During the week beginning June 16, Junior batted .304 and hit 3 homers. He was voted the Northwest League Player of the Week.

For the season, Junior led Bellingham with a .313 average. He also led his team in home runs, with 14; and runs batted in, with 40. He was voted an All-League outfielder, and was selected by the newspaper *Baseball America* as the best major-league prospect in the Northwest League.

During the off-season, everyone agreed that Junior had a bright baseball future. He went on to have another great season in 1988. He spent most of the summer playing for the Mariners' Class A team in San Bernardino, then had a brief stint with its Class AA team in Vermont.

Junior batted .338 with San Bernardino in the California League, and had 11 homers. After being promoted to Vermont in the Eastern League, he batted .279 in 17 games. He then batted .444 in the playoffs.

For the second straight year, Junior achieved star recognition. He was voted to the California League's All-Star team, and once again, *Baseball America* named him the best major-league prospect in his league.

Junior gets a lead off first base.

★ ★ ★

Although invited to the Mariners' spring-training camp in 1989, Junior was not expected to make the team. Only nineteen years old at the time, he was slated to play for the Mariners' AAA team in Calgary. But Junior had other ideas. He batted .359 in spring training, setting records in a number of categories.

"You're my starting center fielder," Mariners' manager Jim Lefebvre finally told Junior. Junior says that those were among the most wonderful words he had ever heard–along with his mom or dad telling him "I love you."

Soon, Mariners' fans grew to love Junior. In his first major-league at bat, he hit a double off Oakland's Dave Stewart. A week later, he homered on the first pitch ever thrown to him at Seattle's Kingdome.

Ken Griffey, Jr., and Jim Lefebvre

Junior and his parents in 1989

That season, Junior—the youngest player in the majors—helped make baseball history with his dad. The two became the first father and son to play in the major leagues at the same time.

"I never dreamed this would happen," said Senior, who, at the time, was again playing with the Cincinnati Reds. "I played in the minors for four-and-a-half years. I thought it would take Junior that long, too."

Lefebvre offered a simple explanation for promoting Junior to the Mariners. "He outplayed a lot of people," Lefebvre explained.

Junior outplayed a lot of people during the season, too. He blasted 16 homers, tied a team record with 8 straight hits, broke a record by reaching base 11 straight times, won a Player of the Week award, and hit safely in 11 straight games. He also had 12 outfield assists and led league outfielders with 6 double plays.

Very likely, Junior also led the league in making telephone calls back home. "I was always calling my parents," he recalls.

Meanwhile, Junior had become so well-known that a candy bar was named after him. The only other baseball player to have had a candy bar named after him was Hall of Famer Reggie Jackson.

In 1990, Junior's play was as sweet as his candy bar. On April 26, he made a fantastic catch, leaping over the fence at Yankee Stadium to rob Jessie Barfield of a homer. Recalling the angry look on Barfield's face, Junior told reporters, "That's why I like playing defense. I get to see somebody else but me get angry." Senior told writers, "I'm in awe, the same as you guys are. I am very proud."

Junior crashes into the wall and holds onto the ball after making a leaping catch to rob an opponent of a hit.

But Ken Griffey, Sr., was never as proud as he was on August 29, 1990, when he signed to play with the Seattle Mariners. With that, he and Junior became the first father and son in baseball history to play together on the same major-league team. Senior played left field; Junior played center field.

The Griffeys are interviewed before their first game as teammates.

Junior and Senior in the outfield

"It was my biggest baseball thrill," says Senior, who had played on two Cincinnati Reds championship teams. Adds Junior, "Nothing has equalled it. The feeling was tremendous." Another special moment occurred when father and son hit back-to-back home runs against California in September 1990.

Junior slams one out of the park.

＊ ＊ ＊

    That season, Junior led the Mariners in home runs with 22, the first time he had hit 20 or more homers in a season. He also batted .300, led the team with 80 RBIs, became the first Mariner elected to the league's All-Star team, and won his first Gold Glove for fielding excellence. Said Mariners coach Gene Clines, "I don't believe anyone has ever been that good at such a young age."

    Junior's performance rose to even higher levels over the next few years. In 1991, he set team records in batting average (.327), doubles, slugging average, and intentional walks. He led the league in grand-slam homers, with 3.

Junior also drove in 100 runs for the first time and, for the second straight year, hit 22 home runs. He won a second-straight Gold Glove Award, and was named by baseball managers as the best fielding outfielder in the league. "He is the brightest thing to come into the majors in years," said Jim Lefebvre, who was now managing the Chicago Cubs.

In 1992, Junior was voted a starter on the American League All-Star team for the third straight year. Although nervous before the game, he went 3 for 3, homered off Cy Young Award-winner Greg Maddux, and was voted the Most Valuable Player in the win over the National League.

Junior and Mariners' owner Jeff Smulyan pose with a framed copy of a magazine cover featuring The Kid.

Junior hit .308 during the season, smacked 27 homers, drove in 103 runs and won his third consecutive Gold Glove. Said Yankees great Don Mattingly, "He does things no one else does. There is no limit to how great he will become."

Junior stealing third base

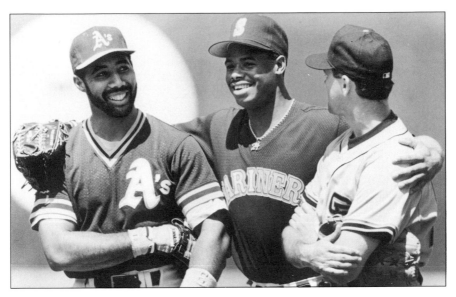
Harold Baines, Ken Griffey, Jr., and Will Clark share a laugh during an All-Star game.

In 1993, Junior had one of the best all-around seasons seen in the big leagues in many years. Voted to the American League All-Star team for his fourth straight year, Junior belted 45 home runs; batted .309; drove in 109 runs; led the league in total bases, with 359; and made only 3 errors out of 327 chances.

He also joined baseball legends Joe DiMaggio, Ted Williams, Ty Cobb, and Mel Ott as the only players to drive in 100 or more runs for three straight years before their 24th birthdays.

During that season, he captured the imagination of baseball fans everywhere by hitting home runs in 8 straight games. This tied a major-league record set by Dale Long of the Pittsburgh Pirates in 1956 and Don Mattingly of the New York Yankees in 1987.

"I'm not disappointed," said Junior, after failing to break the record on July 29 against the Minnesota Twins. "It was fun."

The fun continued in 1994. Throughout the summer, Junior was locked in an intense home-run duel with Chicago's Frank Thomas and Cleveland's Albert Belle. On August 11, Junior hit a grand slam for his 40th home run, which put him ahead of Thomas (38) and Belle (36). That was Griffey's last homer of the season, however. The next day, the major-league players went on strike, and the rest of the 1994 season was canceled. Junior had been on a pace to beat Roger Maris's single-season home-run record of 61.

———— ★ ★ ★ ————

Junior and his wife Melissa live in Renton, Washington. In addition to his brother Craig, who plays in the Mariners organization, Junior has a younger sister, Lathesia.

Although Ken Griffey, Jr., has all the qualities of a superstar, he insists that "being a superstar is nothing I want. I just want to play the game."

"You know who I play for?" he adds. "I play for the kids. If there are kids out there who weren't as lucky as me and they can get some fun out of watching me play, that's great. I play to have fun, and I love to see kids have fun. I love kids. I just like to see them laughing and happy, just as I always want to be."

★ ★ ★

Chronology

1969 – George Kenneth Griffey, Jr., the son of George Kenneth and Alberta Griffey, is born in Donora, Pennsylvania, on November 21.

1979 – Junior begins playing Little League baseball. He bats .1000 and has a pitching record of 12 wins and no losses.

1986 – In his junior year at Moeller High School in Cincinnati, Junior bats .478, hits 10 home runs, and is voted Player of the Year.

1987 – In his senior year, Junior again hits .478. He is voted Player of the Year for the second straight year.
 – The Seattle Mariners make Junior the first selection in the June amateur draft.
 – Assigned to the Mariners' Rookie League team in Bellingham, Washington, Junior bats .313 for the season; *Baseball America* names him the best major-league prospect in the Northwest League.

1988 – Junior has an outstanding season, batting .338 with San Bernardino in Class A, and .279 with Vermont in Class AA. For his play with San Bernardino, he is named by *Baseball America* as the best major-league prospect in the California League.

1989 – Junior is promoted to the Seattle Mariners after an outstanding spring training. He and his dad, Ken Griffey, Sr., become the first father and son to play in the major leagues at the same time.
   – Junior hits a double in his first major-league at bat. He hits 16 home runs during the season, breaks a team record by reaching base 11 straight times, and has 12 outfield assists. A candy bar is named after him.

1990 – After Ken Griffey, Sr., signs with the Mariners in August, Junior and his dad make baseball history by becoming the first father and son to play together on the same major-league team.
   – Junior bats .300, hits 22 homers; becomes the first Mariner voted to the All-Star team, and wins his first Gold Glove.

1991 – Setting a host of team records, Junior bats .327, drives in 100 runs; wins a second straight Gold Glove, and is voted by managers as the best fielding outfielder in the American League.

1992 – Junior is voted a starter on the American League All-Star team for the third straight year. He hits a homer during the game and is voted MVP in the win over the National League.

 – Junior has a season batting average of .308, hits 27 home runs, drives in 103 runs, and wins a Gold Glove for a third straight year.

1993 – Junior ties a major-league record by hitting home runs in 8 straight games. For the season, he bats .309, hits 45 home runs, and becomes one of only five players ever to drive in 100 or more runs three straight years before their 24th birthdays. He is elected to the All-Star game for the fourth straight year.

1994 – Junior clinches his second straight 40-homer season when he cracks number 40 on August 11, the day before the players go on strike and the season ends. For the year, he hits .323 with 90 RBI.

★ ★ ★

About the Author

Howard Reiser has been a well-known New York City newspaper reporter, columnist, and bureau chief. He has also worked as a labor news writer and editor. Today a political speechwriter, Mr. Reiser covered the major news stories in New York City for more than twenty-five years.

Mr. Reiser has written several other books in the *Sports Stars* series. He and his wife, Adrienne, live in New York. They have four children: Philip, Helene, Steven, and Stuart.